A GUIDED JOURNAL
TO
A HEALTHY SENSE OF SELF

Thoughts to inspire peace
within and around the world.

ANTOINETTA VOGELS

BALBOA.PRESS
A DIVISION OF HAY HOUSE

Balboa Press books may be ordered through booksellers or by contacting:

Balboa Press
A Division of Hay House
1663 Liberty Drive
Bloomington, IN 47403
www.balboapress.com
844-682-1282

Because of the dynamic nature of the Internet, any web addresses or links contained in this book may have changed since publication and may no longer be valid. The views expressed in this work are solely those of the author and do not necessarily reflect the views of the publisher, and the publisher hereby disclaims any responsibility for them.

The author of this book does not dispense medical advice or prescribe the use of any technique as a form of treatment for physical, emotional, or medical problems without the advice of a physician, either directly or indirectly. The intent of the author is only to offer information of a general nature to help you in your quest for emotional and spiritual well-being. In the event you use any of the information in this book for yourself, which is your constitutional right, the author and the publisher assume no responsibility for your actions.

Any people depicted in stock imagery provided by Getty Images are models, and such images are being used for illustrative purposes only.
Certain stock imagery © Getty Images.

Edited by Nora Smith
Cover by Marco Scozzi
Illustrations by Laura Vogels

Print information available on the last page.

ISBN: 978-1-9822-6982-1 (sc)
ISBN: 978-1-9822-6983-8 (e)

Balboa Press rev. date: 06/08/2021

HealthySenseOfSelf ®
www.healthysenseofself.com
Email: contact@healthysenseofself.com

Disclaimer

The information in this book is for the purpose of providing inspiration for personal development through gaining self-knowledge and should not be used as psychological, psychiatric, or mental health advice or counselling.

Dedication

To YOU!

You only have one life to live –
make sure it is yours!

Table of contents

Foreword

Dear Reader,

Imagine you are shopping with your best friend, or your spouse, or one of your siblings, or perhaps your childhood nanny. Maybe one or both of your parents have offered to buy you a present and now you are standing inside a dimly lit little shop with a bare bulb glowing from the center of the long narrow space with shelves all the way up to the ceiling. Tucked between a bookstore and a market or café, this dusty old shop could be anywhere in the world: "New York, London, or Bombay. It could be in the suburbs of Cairo, Shanghai, or even in Amsterdam."

The shelves are filled to capacity with rolled-up paper scrolls from all around the world, some new and many quite old. The bearded, ancient-looking man behind the counter welcomes you with a warm smile as he praises his merchandise with love and passion. Your inner security light turns green: you sense you can fully trust this man. He has the face of a person who knows what life is about. As you approach the counter, still a little hesitant, he needs only a slight invitation from you to share his favorite stories.

"All these scrolls contain the pearls of wisdom that I have collected while traveling the world," he starts. "But I won't be here forever and I want *you* to have access to them so that you too can benefit from my lifetime of discoveries."

The scrolls he points at are well-priced and you can see there is something of interest for most anybody. "Please feel free to look around and choose one, for yourself. Then, pick one up to surprise your loved one, and an extra one to treat a beloved family member or friend. I am sure you will find something for your neighbor too."

My dear fellow human being, as you turn the pages of this Guided Journal, imagine yourself in this little shop. Take in the pearls of wisdom, as if each day's thought was one of those scrolls – this time offered to you, not by an intriguing old man but by me, Antoinetta, creator *and experiencer* of the Sense of Self Method. If you trust that "the Universe gives you what you need most" you can even randomly go to a page to see what's there for you today. Sit with that thought for a while. Repeat it throughout the day so that by the end of the day you will have gained a piece of wisdom that can never be taken away from you. Allow it to help you shape your life with more intention.

The quotes in this *Guided Journal to a Healthy Sense of Self* first appeared in the year 2012 as reflections on Facebook. I hope they spark in you an insight and, ultimately, more self-awareness. Those of you who are steady followers of the Healthy Sense of Self Facebook page may even recognize the concepts behind them as they are all based on the Sense of Self Method.

You will come to understand your Self better and better as you use this Guided Journal in the days to come. Study your daily experiences and filter them through the insights of the Sense of Self Method reflected in these quotes. Ask yourself this most important question, "WHY do I do WHAT I do?" The answer to that question will guide you toward restoring your **Sense of Self** and becoming the happiest, healthiest YOU!

To know WHY you do WHAT you do, and what WHAT you do does to you, is a liberating experience. The end result of that deeper knowledge of yourself is inner peace.

That is what I wish for each one of you, personally, and also because it makes our world a better place!

Antoinetta Vogels, Founder Healthy Sense of Self®

Introduction

The Sense of Self (SoS) Method is often used in cases of an emergency, right? Not having a **Healthy Sense of Self** is a sort of existential emergency. But, we all can benefit from acquiring some deeper self-knowledge to help us function better in our complex world.

A **Lack of Sense of Self** can affect almost every area of your life: from stress levels to feeling isolated, from having problems in maintaining relationships to being a good parent to your children, and from anxiety and despair to alcohol problems. It is in those moments that you feel insecure and are unable to ground yourself. People with a Healthy Sense of Self, though, trust themselves and are, therefore, more likely to be successful in whatever they undertake.

Do you constantly feel a solid inner sense of being a "real" person with the right to authentically express who you are? Or do you often feel uneasy or angry for no obvious reason? How frequently do you look for the approval of others to validate your "OK-ness"? Do you maybe need things to be "just so" because you are attached to the outcome of what you are doing? Are you bugged by having to live up to numerous self-imposed conditions that you have to obey at all cost?

How is your sleep?

Healthy Sense of Self – How to be true to your Self and make your world a better place! is the official book about the Sense of Self Method in which you can learn more about it in detail. It is a self-help book, so yes, you can help yourself just by reading it.

The Guided Journal to a Healthy Sense of Self introduces you to the ideas and perspectives of the SoS Method, and helps you get a fresh perspective on your life – it prompts you to think about how the quote for the day applies to you and your life experience.

Why Do Some People Lack a Sense of Self?

(A Summary of the SoS Method)

The key to how children develop that **Natural Sense of Self** lies in the way their primary caretaker relates to them when they are infants. If you are really being "seen and heard" and treated like you are being allowed to be your own person (even when little), you develop an inner sense that "I am myself; I have a right to exist and express who I am."

Often times it happens, though, that your parent, or the person by whom you were raised, unknowingly, sees you as an extension of his or herself. Though they may provide you with food and shelter, you are taught to adapt to their needs and wants at the risk of being ignored, frowned at, or even punished when you are not what your parent needs you to be.

Did you often experience an inner pain, a terror, because the message you got (or still get) from your caregiver(s) tells you: "If you are not the way I want you to be, I will ignore you!" Did you, in the midst of this battle for acknowledgement, accept their approval as the next best thing? Once on that road, getting your caregiver's approval can become compulsive and make you engage in behaviors that are meant to prove to your parent that *you are not what they think you are.*

Then, every time you succeed in pleasing them you **"Feel-good-about-yourself,"** and in the long run that becomes all you really want: "Feel-good-about-yourself," which then functions as a **Substitute Sense of Self** because your real (Sense of) Self is not really there. You are then not home in your own being and that is not only a pity, but unhealthy and dangerous too. Even as an adult you might not know who you really are and end up living for the approval of others because it is the only way you know to minimize the terror of being invisible.

Note that we're not talking about feeling a sense of satisfaction about a job well done or about an encounter that had a desired outcome. People with a healthy Sense of Self have these feelings all the time. It's normal to want to experience feel-good situations in everyday life. The difference is that your very sense of existing *should not depend on getting that approval, and also because it comes with agonizing stress and fear.*

If you recognize that this seemingly harmless need to "Feel-good-about-yourself" means more to you than just being satisfied with your achievements, you might have a problem.

Maybe you even have a **Hidden Agenda** with WHY you do WHAT you do, which is a good reason to investigate your motivations. If you want to be done with lying awake at night and desire a reasonable chance of success in your endeavors, knowing WHY you do WHAT you do will get you the necessary self-knowledge to solve your issues and live happily ever after.

How to Make the Most of This Book

It is said that effecting real change is an inside job. If you are not among the fortunate ones who were given a chance to develop a Sense of Self in a natural, healthy way when you were young, (hey, your parents or caregivers are people too!) you need to do the "inside" work later to claim a **Restored Sense of Self.**

You can use this little book for the next 120 days as part of a simple daily practice to prompt your looking inside – just for the day.

As you are pondering each of these entries, ask yourself the question: **How do I respond to this quote?**

- DO I really *have* to work so hard every day?
- DO I really have to let my partner dominate me as she does?
- DO I need to become the best at all cost?

There are a zillion questions you can pose to yourself, and each one of you will have different ones that help you consider your life more deeply. This book, though, wants to specifically help you find out what it is that makes you "Feel-good-about-yourself." But there is more to it! Ask yourself: Is it a healthy feel-good, or could there be more at stake?

Do you perhaps have a Hidden Goal with what you do, and what could that be? WHO are YOU trying to please and WHY?

Don't be afraid to catalog your thoughts and reactions to the day's message, scribble on the page and in the margins, or in a journal of your choosing, and create an evolving record for yourself that emerges with a little daily attention. What you write in the moment just might surprise you and shed a little light on what makes you YOU! Work with the principles expressed ever so briefly in this book and watch how the SoS Method quietly works to bring insights into your ways of seeing yourself.

This is a pocket-sized book so it is easy to keep with you at all times. Consider it your confidante as you ponder these life questions and challenges. Take *a quiet and undisturbed five minutes for your self, one day at the time.*

When was the last time you took the time to consider how you got to be you and what stops you from living your own life fully and without apology? What might you gently learn if you did spend that time with your Self?

In just 120 days from now you could very well feel much closer to your Natural or Restored Sense of Self. Imagine how that might feel! We all deserve to live our own vibrant life grounded in an inner knowing that we fully have the right to exist, and be who we are because we already ARE in existence!

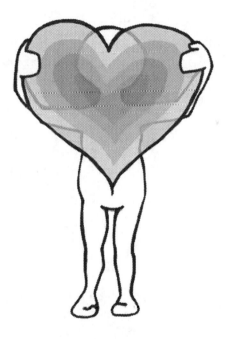

Sense of Self

1

There are two pathways to your future.

One path leads from
the unshakable place of **Real Self**
to a productive and self-fulfilling life;
the other leads
through landmarks of approval
to frenzy, anxiety,
to more frenzy and anxiety and
in the end
to physical, emotional, and mental exhaustion:
disease!

You can switch paths at any time,
but the younger you are
the easier it is.

Make sure you live your life from that place within
where you do not doubt that
you are being YOU.

You may have to dig deeper than you think.

NOTES, THOUGHTS, AND INSIGHTS

PEACE

I can contribute to peace in the world
by managing my "Self."

Managing my Self,
my body, my mind, my emotions,
my own little universe
is a secure way to bring

peace to the world!

NOTES, THOUGHTS, AND INSIGHTS

3

3 KEYS

Here are the three keys
for a world of
Health, Happiness, and Peace:

Be the *Master* of your life

Be the *Manager* of the system called YOU

Be the *Maintenance* person
of Your Body,
Your Mind
and
Your Emotions.

NOTES, THOUGHTS, AND INSIGHTS

4

SELF

You need to *own your* "Self"
so first
you need to know what "Self" actually is.

Self is
my body and what I can do with it –
my mind and what I can do with it –
my emotions - my energy - my spirit –
the gift of life –
the ability to think for myself –
the ability to choose and have an opinion –

the use of my senses –
the option to be alone or with others –
the right to accept or reject
any belief or religion

Can you think of other things that are part of your "Self"?

NOTES, THOUGHTS, AND INSIGHTS

I already AM

The compulsive need to please
comes forth
from craving
acknowledgement
for who and what
YOU are.

What you can do for yourself is
change the habit of believing that you are not worth living.

I do not have to *"earn"* my life!

I already AM

Question to ask yourself:

What do *I* think about this statement

when I think for myself?

NOTES, THOUGHTS, AND INSIGHTS

6

For those of us who have difficulty sleeping

How do you feel about yourself
when you are unable to sleep?

Bad, unhealthy, inadequate, stressed, abnormal?

Are those your own judgments?
Did you think with your own mind?
Are you in the Here and Now?

Or is there someone else
on the screen of your mind?

NOTES, THOUGHTS, AND INSIGHTS

The Magic Formula

Feeling good about ourselves
is a state of being
that allows us to believe, for a moment,
that we are enough.
It is often based on the approval of our caregivers.

Approval that we're addicted to.

In the "Feel-good-about-self" state, scratch the words
"about" and "good."

What's left is: "Feel self."

Sensing your Self is the **Magic Formula** for releasing the
addiction to approval.

Note: Feeling good about yourself can also be a perfectly normal result of
a job well done (when not accompanied by symptoms of overexcitement).

NOTES, THOUGHTS, AND INSIGHTS

"Feel-Good-About-Self"

The Magic Formula

NOTES, THOUGHTS, AND INSIGHTS

For those of us workaholics (1)

Stepping away from work,
as hard as it is,
helps you achieve the freedom
to be yourself.

NOTES, THOUGHTS, AND INSIGHTS

"Feel-good-about-self"

NOTES, THOUGHTS, AND INSIGHTS

9

FREEDOM

To get rid of the addiction to a Substitute Sense of Self,
visualize a safe road and color it green.

On this road you are aware of your body
and what it needs and wants.
You sense who and what you truly are –
anything that overexcites, or over-depresses
is part of a red circle,
the circle of the addiction to approval.

Our brain needs to learn to switch
from being on the red-hot path
of Scoring our small successes
on the way to reaching our **Hidden Goal**
to walking the green path of the Real Self.

Become less dependent on the outcome
of your actions, achievements, or behaviors.

Trade that in for an increasing experience of aspects
of your Real Self.

Know that this life is about YOU
and not about fulfilling all kinds of conditions!

NOTES, THOUGHTS, AND INSIGHTS

DAY
10

For addicts

Addiction is possible only
when YOU are not home in your Self!

As soon as you truly sense your Self

Addiction is over!

Why?
Because with addiction
there is too much
to lose from life.

NOTES, THOUGHTS, AND INSIGHTS

11

Motivation

It is not so much about
WHAT you do but about
WHY you do what you do.

Investigating your **Motivation** is the key to getting to know
yourself thoroughly:
"What am I all about?"

Are your motives healthy
or not?
Is your Motivation
Direct or Indirect?

NOTES, THOUGHTS, AND INSIGHTS

For performing artists

There is a fine line between dedication and compulsion.
The old saying:

"Practice makes perfect"
is valid to a point.

In the end
you play the way you are!

Learning to Sense your Self might give you
the edge you're looking for.

NOTES, THOUGHTS, AND INSIGHTS

Anger

Recognize that
you fear & avoid your own anger
because
being angry doesn't fit your ideal self-image.

Acknowledging your anger
can prevent you from exploding in RAGE.

Also ask yourself:
"Why do I have to live up to that self-image?"
"Why can't I just be me?"

NOTES, THOUGHTS, AND INSIGHTS

Fear of Our Own Anger

We fear our own emotions because they usually do not
contribute to bringing us closer to our Hidden Goal

But it is deadly to our emotional health.
When we skip, avoid, or suppress our own feelings,
we turn into robots.

Take a good look at yourself in the mirror
when you're laughing away uncomfortable feelings.

Ask yourself:
"What do I really feel?
But what is the real reason?
And be totally honest to yourself.

NOTES, THOUGHTS, AND INSIGHTS

DAY
15

There are two groups of people:
people with a Sense of Self
and people
without it.

We're all people – we're all learning,
falling down and growing.

But…

a Lack of Sense of Self
means that
everything you do
is ultimately geared toward
filling in the hole
left by
this Lack of Sense of Self.

It then becomes a matter of life and death.

To succeed
you try to fill that hole.
But it isn't for healthy reasons…
This may be the reason why
what you're doing isn't working.

NOTES, THOUGHTS, AND INSIGHTS

Self-sabotage

What is commonly called "self-sabotage"
is really a symptom
of an active
Substitute Sense of Self-Oriented System.

This symptom
can become the very thing that
points you back in the direction of
your Real Self.

NOTES, THOUGHTS, AND INSIGHTS

Riddle

It doesn't really matter
"WHAT you do" (job or activity),
but "WHAT you do"
does to YOU MATTERS!

NOTES, THOUGHTS, AND INSIGHTS

Healthy Sense of Self

NOTES, THOUGHTS, AND INSIGHTS

Sense of Self Knowledge

We can heal ourselves with Sense of Self knowledge,
thus healing the world.

It'll take a long time
but if we go one step at a time,
one breath at a time,
in this process
our own quality of life
will greatly
increase.

If I do it and you do it, and you, and you... we are
on our way to a better world!

NOTES, THOUGHTS, AND INSIGHTS

Restoring your Sense of Self begins with
getting out of your mind!

Discover that you are not only a mind with
things to do
but
that a big part of you
is your body:
having feet, legs that walk,
hands that can give…

Can you fill in the rest?

NOTES, THOUGHTS, AND INSIGHTS

A question to those who need it:
Is it okay to be about yourself?

"Am I not
the King or Queen
of my own universe?"

Is each one of us not living in our own bubble?

Occasionally,
we want to visit someone else in their domain
or let somebody into ours.

How big is the space we may (want to) take up
in other people's bubbles?
a friend's,
a spouse's,
a son's or daughter's?

NOTES, THOUGHTS, AND INSIGHTS

Ego-References (1)

Having **Ego-References**
is a condition that is based on your
Early Childhood Survival Strategy.

While observing your caregiver,
when you were a toddler:
"How do I have to be or what do I have to do
so they give me something
that looks like
love?"

Make a list of your Ego-References and you're on your way
to freeing yourself from them.

NOTES, THOUGHTS, AND INSIGHTS

Ego-References (2)

If keeping your house clean
is a compulsion
that you need to do
to
Feel-good-about-yourself,
chances are that
keeping your house clean
is a **Vehicle** you use
to show off
your Ego-Reference
of "being neat and organized."

Your Hidden Agenda then is to show your
caregiver/parent
that you are better than he/she thinks.

Your Hidden Goal might be to finally feel
accepted and acknowledged,
which then functions as
your
Substitute Sense of Self.

NOTES, THOUGHTS, AND INSIGHTS

Ego-References (3)

If being on time
is charged with feelings of anxiety, frenzy,
and stress,
chances are that
"being on time"
is an Ego-Reference for you.

Your Hidden Agenda is to show your caregiver
that,
contrary to what they think,
you CAN be on time.

You hope that,
by succeeding in living up to that Ego-Reference,
your caregiver will finally accept and acknowledge
you
as the beloved son or daughter
you so desperately
want to be.

NOTES, THOUGHTS, AND INSIGHTS

More on Ego-References

An Ego-Reference is
compulsive need to show
your parent/caregiver
or even your self,
that you can do specific things better
than he or she thinks.

Ego-References only exist
if you are addicted to your caregiver's approval!
They form the cornerstones of **Indirect Motivation** and the
entire Substitute Sense of Self-Oriented System
which kicks in when there is

a Lack of Sense of Self!

NOTES, THOUGHTS, AND INSIGHTS

25

Stress & Fear

Everyday fear and stress in normal amounts
is called, in the SoS Method,
Quality-of-Life level stress or fear.

It is normal to experience apprehension or a
degree of stress on a daily basis.

As long as the fear and stress isn't experienced
as a matter of life and death.

In other words,

as long as your Sense of Self doesn't depend on it.

NOTES, THOUGHTS, AND INSIGHTS

Satisfaction

Feeling good about yourself on a Quality-of Life level
is a normal and healthy experience.

It is perfectly fine to feel satisfied with
a job well done.

As long as it is not compulsive and a "must have"
at all cost.

As long as your Sense of Self doesn't depend on it;
as long as "feeling-good-about-yourself"
doesn't define
who you are or even
THAT you are.

NOTES, THOUGHTS, AND INSIGHTS

Honesty

Being absolutely honest with yourself
is crucial
when working on
Restoring your Sense of Self.

Make sure you recognize denial of
your true Motivation
at all times.

Have the courage to face yourself!
Don't fool yourself!

NOTES, THOUGHTS, AND INSIGHTS

"WHY do I do WHAT I do?"
"WHY do I want WHAT I want?"

"Is that answer true if I am totally honest with myself?"

"Is there possibly another reason?"

"Do I actively agree with that motivation when
I think about it for myself?"
"Where does that idea come from anyway?"

Thoroughly questioning your Motivation
is a very powerful tool in learning
to understand yourself.

Understanding where you come from
is necessary to be able to change direction
toward the one you wish to go.

NOTES, THOUGHTS, AND INSIGHTS

King or Queen

Each one of us is
the KING or QUEEN of ourr own universe.
This thought implies that

WE are the rulers over OUR kingdom,
which implies that
we allow OTHERS have the FREEDOM
to rule over
THEIR kingdoms.

This way a peaceful world becomes
a possibility.

NOTES, THOUGHTS, AND INSIGHTS

30

I exist already

When I truly sense my Self,
my breathing,
my heartbeat,
my pain,

I should know that I don't depend
on the outcome of any activity,
nor on what other people think of me.
Why would I?
I AM already,
otherwise I wouldn't be able to sense these things.

Maybe pain is there to make us aware of that…?

NOTES, THOUGHTS, AND INSIGHTS

31

How to be your Self?

Actively notice all aspects of your Self,

embrace them,
and interpret them as proof of your existence.

You ARE already (existing)

and you have got everything in place
to be your Self.

Eliminate all desire to be different
from who and what you are.

NOTES, THOUGHTS, AND INSIGHTS

32

Are you afraid of your own feelings?

Feelings often present themselves
in moments that you do not want them
because you're working
a different agenda!

When we're not dependent
on the outcome of our jobs, actions,
or behavior for our Sense of Self,
there is room for our emotions
and we do not have to be afraid of them.

NOTES, THOUGHTS, AND INSIGHTS

Early Childhood Decisions

Did you know that
it is quite possible that
you think your life is about YOU
but that
in reality
you have created your life based upon
making your "Early Childhood" decisions
work no matter what

Why?
Because to feel
like you are
SOMEBODY depends on their success!

Can you think of some of your Early Childhood decisions?

Why were they so important to you?

Do they still serve you in the present?

NOTES, THOUGHTS, AND INSIGHTS

A Reconditioning Journey

I am
first and foremost
a person.

That means
I am my very own unique,
independent,
autonomous human being.

First there is
"I AM"
then comes
"I do."

"I AM not my doing
thought…
I need my BEING for doing.
Fortunately, I can just be
without doing."

NOTES, THOUGHTS, AND INSIGHTS

Addiction

The ultimate cause of (any) addiction lies in a
Lack of Sense of Self.

Restoring your Sense of Self
is crucial
for any recovery to last.

NOTES, THOUGHTS, AND INSIGHTS

To Be Seen and Heard

When you have a Lack of Sense of Self

chances are
you are just running around
trying to live up to all the conditions you have imposed on
yourself…

They're based on

how your caregiver (parent) needed you to be
because you thought

that by being more "so"
or doing more of "that"
your caregiver might look at you in a more positive way
and may even "see" you.

NOTES, THOUGHTS, AND INSIGHTS

Lack of Sense of Self

NOTES, THOUGHTS, AND INSIGHTS

DAY

37

Who I really am
(my Self)

is not dependent
on the outcome of my achievements
or
on what others think of me.

I think with my own mind and feel with my own heart.

NOTES, THOUGHTS, AND INSIGHTS

38

Survival System

A Survival System is there to help us survive.

To replace it with a new one
feels like a threat to the system,
so it defends itself heavily,
in its attempt to protect us.

Understand that and be gentle with yourself
when it comes to changing old habits.

Gentle but persistent!

NOTES, THOUGHTS, AND INSIGHTS

Heritage

Developing your own set of values
instead of
working off the ones you have inherited
creates the difference
between
doubting and trusting
yourself.

NOTES, THOUGHTS, AND INSIGHTS

What is it that keeps us captivated
by the idea
of having to reach a specific goal at all cost?

What is your specific goal that you need to realize?

What will that get you in the end?

Be aware that nothing really changes for yourself: you will
still be a mortal human being.

NOTES, THOUGHTS, AND INSIGHTS

Think for Yourself

What do we base our decisions on?

On what used to be relevant in the past?
or
on what is relevant in the present?

How to know the difference?

Activate your own little grey cells
instead of
automatically
diving into that bag filled with past values.

They may not even be yours!

NOTES, THOUGHTS, AND INSIGHTS

You Live the Way You Are

The quality of your interior
is responsible for
the quality of your exterior!

Get to know yourself!

Watering the roots of your inner plant
makes it possible
for you to grow and blossom!

NOTES, THOUGHTS, AND INSIGHTS

DAY
43

Anxiety happens when
what you thought was good for you
is threatened by outside circumstances,

OR IF YOU TO CHANGE YOUR MIND ABOUT IT.

So hang in there and break through the anxiety…
DO IT ANYWAY
well-being is waiting on the other side.

Freeing yourself from the habit
of living up to certain conditions
and
being able to access your own life
can be anxiety provoking
– in the beginning.

But there is the reward of truly living your own life!

NOTES, THOUGHTS, AND INSIGHTS

A Healthy Sense of Self
is the backbone of the human psyche.

Without it,
a person skips their own life
altogether.

NOTES, THOUGHTS, AND INSIGHTS

Inspiring
each and every individual
to get
a healthy Sense of Self
for themselves
and for their children
is

my contribution to

World Peace!

Will you help me?

NOTES, THOUGHTS, AND INSIGHTS

Hidden Goal

NOTES, THOUGHTS, AND INSIGHTS

46

Restored Sense of Self

Let us all work on Restoring our Sense of Self,
men and women,
adults and children
alike!

When we have a healthy Sense of Self, we know we do
not need what somebody else has
to make us feel better about ourselves.

We are all the same, yet, we have certain attributes that
are unique.

It takes a Healthy Sense of Self to celebrate diversity!

NOTES, THOUGHTS, AND INSIGHTS

I want to be myself!
You want to be yourself.
He wants to be himself.
She wants to be herself.
We want to be ourselves.
They want to be themselves!

We all want and need to be able to be ourselves!

So let's work on
restoring or strengthening our Sense of Self
because
it takes a healthy Sense of Self
to fully be yourself.

NOTES, THOUGHTS, AND INSIGHTS

DAY
48

Here is the short answer to the question

"Why do some people never get depressed
while others do?"

Because they have a healthy Sense of Self and people who
are depressed do not have
a Sense of Self!

So work on your Restored Sense of Self!

NOTES, THOUGHTS, AND INSIGHTS

DAY
49

How do you get access to your very own life?

By freeing yourself from the addiction to a
Substitute Sense of Self.

There is a dependency on
"Feeling-good-about-yourself"
because
it functions as a Substitute Sense of Self.

It is based on
approval.

Restore your Sense of Self!
Be in and with your body
Think for yourself
Know WHY you do WHAT you do!

That gives you freedom from the addiction to approval…

Now you can be true to your Self.

NOTES, THOUGHTS, AND INSIGHTS

Do you want to find a natural,
cheap, and fun way
to be more successful?

Learn to fully be YOURSELF!
The results are:

You don't depend on outcomes
for your Sense of Self

You know what you want

You know your strengths and weaknesses

You are there for others

You work but don't forget to live

You have healthy vibes and energy

People trust you!

NOTES, THOUGHTS, AND INSIGHTS

With a Natural or a Restored Sense of Self
you are so fortunate
because

you are able to spend your time
doing something you really like
or that needs to be done
and the odds are
that you are going to be successful!

For all, less fortunate, others... you too can learn
to be that way!

How?
Know that all of us have challenges in our lives!

If lacking a Sense of Self is one of yours,
we can help you get over it.

NOTES, THOUGHTS, AND INSIGHTS

52

Direct Motivation

The reason why some people are successful:

Having the right Motivation,
that is what it's all about.
The SoS Method calls it
Direct Motivation.

When your intention is not convoluted
by Hidden Goals
the Universe gets the picture
and things
will fall into place.

NOTES, THOUGHTS, AND INSIGHTS

Group-identity

Have you ever wondered how *a group* can function
as an "extended self"?

In tribal times
we used *belonging to a group*
as a place to be safer,
because human beings used to be so vulnerable.

But in our day and age we need to step it up,
take responsibility for our own body/life
and let others do the same.

Belonging to a group
should not encourage dependency
or a need for acceptance.

If only we could move
from dependency to independency to interdependency

It could be the beginning of moving toward

World Peace.

NOTES, THOUGHTS, AND INSIGHTS

54

Are those thoughts really yours?

A great way of starting to
Restore your Sense of Self
is by learning to see
that not all your thoughts are your own.

Unconsciously,
you may have adopted many of your
parents'/caregivers' judgments
about things and people
and even about yourself.

And like many of us
you may still be working hard
to improve yourself based on those judgments
so that you don't have the time

to live your own life!

NOTES, THOUGHTS, AND INSIGHTS

Substitute Sense of Self

NOTES, THOUGHTS, AND INSIGHTS

DAY
55

Parental mix-up

Did you ever consider
that some parent(s) want you, their child,
to be "just so,"
not because it is so much better,
but because it is more convenient for them?

Subconsciously, they wanted you
to not be present as a "real" person,
as your self

but

as *an extension* of them!

That way you would positively contribute
to their Substitute Sense of Self
and they had more time and energy
to work on their own issues.

NOTES, THOUGHTS, AND INSIGHTS

Being dependent on the outcome of our activities
or on what others think of us…

That has been the human condition
until now for many of us.

Now it is time
we take responsibility for ourselves
and start by discovering
what we truly think of things
once we learn
to think for ourselves

"What are my (own) values and criteria?"

"What do I think about it myself?"

"What is my own opinion?"

"How do I see it?"

"What purpose do I want my life to have?"

NOTES, THOUGHTS, AND INSIGHTS

57

Dependency to Approval

The habit
of being dependent on the approval of your parents
to "Feel-good-about-yourself"
transfers to being dependent
on the approval
of other qualifying individuals.

NOTES, THOUGHTS, AND INSIGHTS

To sacrifice yourself
or not to sacrifice yourself

How much of your life, of yourself,
are you willing to sacrifice for your loved one(s)?

When is it sacrifice?
When is it dependency?
And when is it an act of wisdom
to yield to your partner's wishes?

That is the question!

NOTES, THOUGHTS, AND INSIGHTS

59

Living in harmony

If you really want to make it work,
living in harmony with your family,
with your brothers and sisters, with your parents,
each one has to stick to
being his or herself
while allowing the others to do the same!

NOTES, THOUGHTS, AND INSIGHTS

DAY
60

Motivation Check

Questioning your Motivation
is a very powerful tool
for getting to know yourself.

Understanding where you come from
is necessary to be able
to change your direction toward
where you wish to go.

NOTES, THOUGHTS, AND INSIGHTS

DAY
61

Regrets of the Dying

Remember that sooner or later
your
(and my)
life
is going to come to an end.

Would there be anything more dramatic
than this last minute awareness
that you haven't really lived
your own life?

Each one of us is individually responsible
for being truly alive.

NOTES, THOUGHTS, AND INSIGHTS

A Healthy Sense of Self
is what it takes to fully be yourself.

When you are yourself
you stand a much better chance
to stay free
from the many problems that plague us in our day and age:

relationship problems,
problems with learning (children/young adults),
problems with addiction,
or with money,
self-sabotage,
fear of failure,
(domestic-) violence,
suicide,
and even

acts of war!

NOTES, THOUGHTS, AND INSIGHTS

Building a Healthy Sense of Self
is the one and only way
each one of us
can truly contribute to
WORLD PEACE!

If we acknowledge ourselves as unique, independent,
and autonomous human beings
with the right to existence
for the mere fact that
we already exist;
if we agree that
we have the right to our own preferences,
tastes, and emotions
and the choice to express them
we cannot but let that ALSO be true for others.

Now there suddenly is a lot less reason

for war!

NOTES, THOUGHTS, AND INSIGHTS

Restored Sense of Self

NOTES, THOUGHTS, AND INSIGHTS

64

For those of us workaholics (2)

Do you have great trouble deleting something
from your overly full to-do list?

In that case, you might want to ask yourself
what you perceive to be at stake.

Is it really about the issue at hand?
Or does your need to get things done tie in with
a Hidden Agenda
deep down in yourself
that you are not really aware of,
let alone are willing to admit?

Self-knowledge is power.

NOTES, THOUGHTS, AND INSIGHTS

Day
65

We are all busy as hell

BUT

Transformation
and beginning a new
is possible
each moment of the day.

Change is just one decision away.

NOTES, THOUGHTS, AND INSIGHTS

For those of us who have relapsed

Relapsing in being dependent on a
Substitute Sense of Self
means falling back on the automatic pilot
that we allow (again)
to govern our lives.

Signs and symptoms:
anxiety and frenzy about
not being able to fulfill the demanding tasks
or live up to certain conditions.

You might not be able to sleep
Maybe you're always be in a hurry…

STOP RELAPSE
and renew your awareness that your life is yours
and
that you are free
to do what YOU want
and be YOURSELF.

NOTES, THOUGHTS, AND INSIGHTS

Why do some people have a (natural)
Healthy Sense of Self
while others end up with
a Lack of Sense of Self,
which makes them dependent on a
Substitute Sense of Self?

Possibly their parents were able
to mirror back to them
that they count as a real person by truly seeing them.

Parents, do relate to your children
as true individuals
who are their own person
who have their own voice.

By making your children feel
that they count
you enable them to develop
a healthy sense of themselves.

The best gift in life!

NOTES, THOUGHTS, AND INSIGHTS

68

Shared responsibility

As a driver, I used to think that making sure
not to run into other cars
was totally my responsibility…

Until I saw that it is other people's jobs as well
to watch out and
not bump into my car.

Similarly,
I am not the only one responsible
for quarrels and disagreements that get out of hand –
we share that responsibility with all others
who are participating in the conversation,
who share our lives.

What a relief that I do not have to carry that burden
all by myself!

NOTES, THOUGHTS, AND INSIGHTS

Lower your risks (1)

Working your way up
to a Healthy Sense of Self
leads to better general health

so

you will be less stressed out
and therefore less affected by
the attacks
of bugs and bacteria on your body

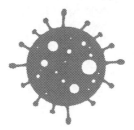

NOTES, THOUGHTS, AND INSIGHTS

DAY
70

Lower your risks (2)

Working your way up to
a Healthy Sense of Self
leads to functioning better on the job.

You are under less stress.

So
you are less likely to be affected by
stress/job-related injuries.

Professional musicians:
less muscle tension due to stress!

NOTES, THOUGHTS, AND INSIGHTS

71

For us over-eaters and over-drinkers

Here is a cheap remedy against
overeating as well as
substance abuse.

We tend to want to eat and drink after work,
as a sort of reward for the work that we did that day.

When we make sure
we have a Direct Motivation
with what we are
doing,
our activity/job brings us satisfaction,
which is the reward
and we don't have those cravings
when we are done.

NOTES, THOUGHTS, AND INSIGHTS

DAY
72

Stop procrastinating!

Find out
what really makes your heart sing!

STOP being the slave
of your automatic pilot's agenda
and feel the burden weighing on your shoulders.

Ask yourself:

What gives me joy?

DO IT!

NOTES, THOUGHTS, AND INSIGHTS

TRICKY

So often
we tend to use our healing
to persevere with even more tenacity
in making the mistakes that cause our pain
in the first place.

We think
we know what is good for us
better
than Nature.

Are you ready to give up
what hasn't worked so far
or
do you intend to use your healing
to make
what you were trying to achieve
work after all?

NOTES, THOUGHTS, AND INSIGHTS

DAY
74

Restored Sense of Self

When you have worked your way up to a
Restored Sense of Self
you can finally
become playful (again)
and enjoy life.

Play an instrument,
sing,
play a sport,
go hiking or sightseeing,
help a friend,
be with your family... or write a book.

Finally you understand why some people can be
so happy
because now you can be happy too!

NOTES, THOUGHTS, AND INSIGHTS

Direct Motivation

NOTES, THOUGHTS, AND INSIGHTS

Day

75

For those of us over-eaters

There are five reasons to eat:

to feed yourself,
to indulge yourself,
to ground yourself,
to reward yourself,
to release anger by moving your jaws.

When you have a Healthy Sense of Self,
only the one good reason
sticks with you!

NOTES, THOUGHTS, AND INSIGHTS

Have you ever wondered
why you always have to work until you
"Feel-good-about-self"
at all cost?

Shouldn't you always feel good about yourself?

Is it really because you want to feel satisfied
about what you did,
or about the way you did it?

Or does it go much deeper?

Is it maybe a sort of ultimate reward
you are compulsively driven to get
with what you do or
with how you behave?

It might be time to Restore your Sense of Self.
Know that you already ARE
and that the outcome of your actions or behaviors
dosn't make you a different person.

NOTES, THOUGHTS, AND INSIGHTS

For us pacifists

How many of the people you know actually
seem to know themselves,
and how many truly are being themselves?

If we are not brought up with
a Healthy Sense of Self,
it is a skill we need to acquire.

For many of us becoming truly true to our Self
happens when we are deep into our adulthood
and learning how to do that
proves more work than we ever imagined.

But once we've got it,
we've bridged the gap between
the old and the new world.

Now we are able to educate our children in such
a way that they can become their own person.

And once you have what it takes to be yourself,
there is no reason left
for war.

NOTES, THOUGHTS, AND INSIGHTS

For those of us who are insecure

How about we change that haunting question
that expresses our ongoing insecurity:

"What if I can't do it…?" into
"What if I CAN do it…?" just like that.

Let the eternal doubt that
an unfortunate parent has instilled in us
be the dead-end street that we have to learn to avoid.

It is just a conditioned reflex-thought.

Let us practice this new road of changing our belief in
"What if I can do it…?"
and we will find
it opens a new world.

NOTES, THOUGHTS, AND INSIGHTS

For those of us workaholics (3)

How tempting it is
to identify completely
with your professional activity or job!

Don't you "Feel-good-about-yourself"
when you have done something well?
Are you driven to get that feeling back?

If the compulsion is too strong
you'd better ask yourself:
"who am I WITHOUT that feeling?"

It is crucial to find out
if you're maybe addicted to it.

Note: feeling good about yourself
as a Quality-of-Life validation
is perfectly fine.
There is nothing wrong
with feeling satisfied about a job well done.

NOTES, THOUGHTS, AND INSIGHTS

80

To all of us

Hey, we're in this together!

If we all work out our own issues
we won't be envious, greedy, defensive,
or arrogant anymore
because

we (already) have what it takes to be ourselves.

Greetings to all of you:
We are the same
as well as
uniquely different!

NOTES, THOUGHTS, AND INSIGHTS

Finding your Self

At first, I had no idea
who I was,
what "Self" meant,
where to find it,
or how to connect to it.

It took me about thirty years to discover it.

Now you can learn what I found out
and use it to your benefit:
Restore your Sense of Self
by
reading the book
Healthy Sense of Self – The secret to being your best Self,
doing the course.

It'll help you help yourself
to live your life for yourself
and truly be of service to others!

NOTES, THOUGHTS, AND INSIGHTS

DAY
82

You are present to your Self when:

- you are present in your body
- you are directly connected to your own being
- you use your own mind
- you are living in the Here and Now
- you take others for who they are
- your conversations occur to convey information
  or for the fun of it
- your work is about getting
  from A to B or Z or for your enjoyment
- your life is not "a performance"
- you are conscious of your senses
- you know that the danger of slipping back
  into automatic pilot is always lurking
- you are able to validate your existence
  as temporary and precious
- you are able to be with others in a non-needy way.

NOW you are also ready to be part of and contribute to
a healthy community!

NOTES, THOUGHTS, AND INSIGHTS

Be determined to do your inner work
and Restore your Sense of Self.
It is the best gift you can give yourself
as well as
contribute to a better world!

You are born with that potential.

But you need the right feedback
at the right time to develop it properly.

With the wrong feedback or no feedback at all
your Sense of Self
becomes
like a crooked tree
and just like that tree
you might wither away.

You have to help yourself and straighten
your misshapen Sense of Self
so it'll allow you to develop
the majestic blueprint of your soul
and live your life to your fullest potential.

NOTES, THOUGHTS, AND INSIGHTS

Indirect Motivation

NOTES, THOUGHTS, AND INSIGHTS

84

Struggle for life

The force that is needed
to become present to yourself
and Restore your Sense of Self
is comparable to the life and death fight
of an antilope in the claws of a lion.

NOTES, THOUGHTS, AND INSIGHTS

85

Living from the head up

Our Sense of Self
starts with awareness of our body.

Too often
we are so absorbed by the things we do
we hardly experience our body.

It is as if we are a floating brain
that needs to succeed
in its task at hand
at all cost.

NOTES, THOUGHTS, AND INSIGHTS

DAY
86

Body-awareness

How to gain more awareness of your body?

Mention out loud
all the various body parts,
organs and
bodily functions
you can discover in and of your body.

Add to it
your mind,
your emotions,
the energy that is given to you.

Some people may want to include "your spirit."

All of that is YOU
and there is no need to fulfill any conditions
to enjoy that!

NOTES, THOUGHTS, AND INSIGHTS

Our Sense of Self is
the backbone of our psyche;
without it
we are a pudding.

NOTES, THOUGHTS, AND INSIGHTS

Working on your Self…
what does it really mean?

Introspection,
looking within,
finding out what you are all about,
asking yourself:
"For what do I get out of my bed in the morning!?"

What IS your ultimate Motivation?

If the answer you get
does not please you,
do something about it!

Get one that does.
One that makes your life worthwhile.

NOTES, THOUGHTS, AND INSIGHTS

You only have one life to live.

Make sure
it is your own!

NOTES, THOUGHTS, AND INSIGHTS

DAY
90

Being connected to
and having awareness of

YOUR BODY

is a must
if you want to be totally yourself.

Your body forms a large percentage of YOU.

What/who would you be
without your body?

NOTES, THOUGHTS, AND INSIGHTS

91

To us parents and children

What do all people have in common?

Yes, we all have parents or caregivers.

We are raised and educated
by people who are
most of the time
just as insecure and needy as we are;

they only look older.

NOTES, THOUGHTS, AND INSIGHTS

To us children!

Parents are people too!

In their neediness and insecurity
they do not always make the best choices
or behave the correct way.

So start trusting your own opinion and judgment

but
make sure first
that it is truly your own.

NOTES, THOUGHTS, AND INSIGHTS

Hidden Agenda

NOTES, THOUGHTS, AND INSIGHTS

To us parents!

Help
reduce hate
in the world
by
allowing your sons and daughters
to flourish
and be
themselves.

Be there for them
totally,
the full 100%.

Acknowledge their presence in this world.
Show them you really see them
accept them as who they are
so they can develop
a Healthy Sense of Self
and have a life of their own!

NOTES, THOUGHTS, AND INSIGHTS

Running your own show

Think for yourself
and
make sure
that
there is nobody else
"on the screen of your mind,"
pulling the strings of your thoughts,
calling the shots in the game of your life.

Look at the world and use your own
uncontaminated, fresh
judgment.

NOTES, THOUGHTS, AND INSIGHTS

DAY
95

The moment you are
truly yourself
while expressing
your opinion,
you feel balanced
and
free of fear or frenzy.

No anxious heartbeats or
sweaty palms
because
you know
you don't depend on
what you do or what you say
for your
Sense of Self.

NOTES, THOUGHTS, AND INSIGHTS

My life is mine!

Make sure you are
in the Here and Now.

Make sure there is
nobody else who whispers in your ear
how to behave and
what to choose…

"Thank you…
this is my body
and my life."

"I will make
my own decisions."

NOTES, THOUGHTS, AND INSIGHTS

How to Be Yourself

Acknowledge yourself presently
as a unique,
independent human being,
even if your caregivers
were unable to do so in the past.

You already have what it takes
to be yourself
and that is all you have to do
in this world.

By doing so
you even help
the world become
a
better place!

NOTES, THOUGHTS, AND INSIGHTS

Look at the trees,
they are all different yet the same.

Your brain is like a tree;
chains of neurons have developed into permanent shapes
like branches of a tree.

If we could lift our skulls
and clearly see what the specific areas are
that are flourishing and which parts
struggle to see the daylight.

No doubt
we would have more compassion
for ourselves
as well
as for others.

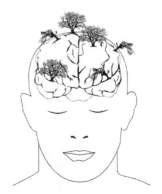

NOTES, THOUGHTS, AND INSIGHTS

I invite you all

to draw
your own brain-tree.

What will it look like?
Which side is well-balanced,
which one under-developed,
or even absent?

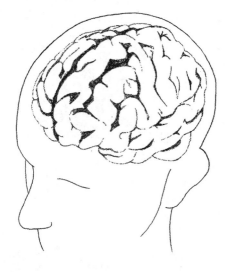

NOTES, THOUGHTS, AND INSIGHTS

100

It is much easier
to have a Healthy Sense of Self
when you are by yourself
than
in the midst of a crowd.

Now that we know that,
we may want to pay attention
to not losing our
Sense of Self
when with friends or family!

NOTES, THOUGHTS, AND INSIGHTS

A Sense of Self
is a joy
forever…

that is,
if it is
healthy!

NOTES, THOUGHTS, AND INSIGHTS

Ego-References

NOTES, THOUGHTS, AND INSIGHTS

A bit of theory

Ego-Reference
is a term used in the
SoS Method.

Ego-references are rules
that you have imposed on yourself
to live by or
live up to
because you noticed,
as a young child,
that your caregiver approved of you,
which made you,
and still makes you

"Feel-good-about-yourself."

NOTES, THOUGHTS, AND INSIGHTS

Ask yourself:

"Why do I do this work?"
"Why do I want to achieve this goal?"

If the answer is:
"so I get my caregiver's approval,
which
makes me 'Feel-good-about-myself,'"

you need to learn
to think with your own mind.

Determine your own values
and live up to them!

NOTES, THOUGHTS, AND INSIGHTS

How do we build a healthy sense of self?
How do we restore our sense of self?

Step 1*

Ask yourself
whether you are
truly in touch with your body
or
if you are mainly concerned about
the things in your head…

The work that needs to be done…
The people that need to be kept at peace
with you – or with each other –
or any of the other worries
that are specific to
you?

* For these Steps see *The Twelve SoS Reconditioning Statements* at
  pp. 296, 297.

NOTES, THOUGHTS, AND INSIGHTS

105

How do we build a healthy sense of self?
How do we restore our sense of self?

Step 2

Try to establish
a direct connection
with yourself, as well as with
things, people, and events.

In other words:
Make sure your actions, activities, and behaviors
are not Vehicles
for a Substitute Sense of Self,
that manifests itself as
the desired state of
"Feeling-good-about-yourself."

NOTES, THOUGHTS, AND INSIGHTS

How do we build a healthy sense of self?
How do we restore our sense of self?

Step 3

Be serious about finding out
who the other person is who occupies your mind.

Is it truly your own opinion,
judgment, or criteria
that you use to validate your own behavior?

If not, then who is it?

Kick them out!

NOTES, THOUGHTS, AND INSIGHTS

107

How do we build a healthy sense of self?
How do we restore our sense of self?

Step 4

Be in the "Here and Now"
as opposed to
being "in a trance,"
in the past,

compensating for
the missed building blocks of the development of a
Healthy Sense of Self:

ACKNOWLEDGE YOURSELF
as a separate, unique human being
with your own life,
your own karma,
your own tastes, preferences, and opinions!

NOTES, THOUGHTS, AND INSIGHTS

How do we build a healthy sense of self?
How do we restore our sense of self?

Step 5

Actively listen to the person you are talking with.

Make sure you truly see him for the person he is.
Make sure you truly see her for the person she is.

Make sure your automatic pilot
doesn't mistake that person
for a specific person from your past
with whom you have
unfinished business!

NOTES, THOUGHTS, AND INSIGHTS

Vehicle

NOTES, THOUGHTS, AND INSIGHTS

How do we build a healthy sense of self?
How do we restore our sense of self?

Step 6

When in conversation with others
observe yourself
and notice what your goal is.

Do not endlessly prolong the conversation
trying to end up with a result that makes you
"Feel-good-about-yourself."

Give priority
to the content
of your conversation, over
your need to get to the state of

"Feel-good-about-self."

NOTES, THOUGHTS, AND INSIGHTS

DAY
110

How do we build a healthy sense of self?
How do we restore our sense of self?

Step 7

Make sure you actually are able to
STOP working
when you feel like doing something else!

Counter the compulsion
to go on
until you are

"Feeling-good-about-self."

Note that your true Motivation
might not be
about WHAT you are doing but
about WHY you are doing it.

Find out what keeps you spell bound or else,
you run the risk to skip your life altogether!

NOTES, THOUGHTS, AND INSIGHTS

DAY
111

How do we build a healthy sense of self?
How do we restore our sense of self?

Step 8

Make absolutely sure that your life has not become

a performance.

Make sure you are really *living it*.

NOTES, THOUGHTS, AND INSIGHTS

How do we build a healthy sense of self?
How do we restore our sense of self?

Step 9

I am consciously aware in using my senses.

I AM because
I watch and I truly see;
I AM because
I listen and I truly hear;
I AM because
I smell and I take in and appreciate what I smell;
I AM because
I feel how the grass touches my bare feet;
I AM because
I taste the honey and enjoy having that ability.

I listen so I AM – I see so I AM – I smell so I AM –
I taste so it must be that I EXIST.
I feel/sense so I EXIST.
I sense my Self.

NOTES, THOUGHTS, AND INSIGHTS

113

How do we build a healthy sense of self?
How do we restore our sense of self?

Step 10

After recovering
from the addiction to a
Substitute Sense of Self,
I know it,
relapse is always lurking

I am utterly aware of it.

When it happens
I am gentle with myself
but determined
to get back
on the path
to
a healthy sense of self.

NOTES, THOUGHTS, AND INSIGHTS

DAY
114

How do we build a healthy sense of self?
How do we restore our sense of self?

Step 11

Now that I have my Self available for myself
I am ready
to share my life with others.

Only when we are emotionally independent
we can be interdependent in a healthy way
and build that ideal community,
and create
a better world.

NOTES, THOUGHTS, AND INSIGHTS

How do we build a healthy sense of self?
How do we restore our sense of self?

Step 12

When I sense myself
I can be myself.

Now I don't depend on others to be happy!
I am relaxed,

I have no Hidden Goals.

Now that I live for my Self,
mentally, emotionally, and physically
when I GIVE,
i can give
unconditionally
because
now
I give to be of service.

A healthy community is formed by
people with a
strong sense of self.

NOTES, THOUGHTS, AND INSIGHTS

WE, people
with a healthy Sense of Self
have no need to fight others
for fear that they will take away
our opportunity
to "Feel-good-about-ourselves."

We don't have to get that feeling from outside!
Feeling good about ourselves
is our default state.

NOTES, THOUGHTS, AND INSIGHTS

117

If there is a big discrepancy
between
what you need to do
and
what you want to do,
you're lucky.

Most people don't know what they want.

Honor your Self
and don't do
what you "should" do
but
make sure you do what you really
want or *need*
to do!

NOTES, THOUGHTS, AND INSIGHTS

Day
118

Self-knowledge
is
a powerful tool

AGAINST WAR!

NOTES, THOUGHTS, AND INSIGHTS

Which story do you choose?

I want the world to be perfect so
I can make my caregiver(s) happy and then
maybe they will see me and
acknowledge me for the person I am.
Maybe I will be treated as a real and normal person.

OR

I have the courage
to admit that the world is far from perfect,
so I can allow myself to not be perfect,
so I can enjoy others
without being judgmental
and
actually
have friends!

NOTES, THOUGHTS, AND INSIGHTS

Hey people with a Healthy Sense of Self!

Do you happen to know
someone in your environment
whose Sense of Self is not so strong?

If each one of us would commit
to helping
that one person we know,
to move from
a Lack of Sense of Self
to
a Restored Sense of Self
by
introducing him or her
to the Sense of Self Method

…You would certainly get
good karma points!

NOTES, THOUGHTS, AND INSIGHTS

NOTES, THOUGHTS, AND INSIGHTS

NOTES, THOUGHTS, AND INSIGHTS

Glossary

Annihilation

A strong perception of being overlooked, not being seen and heard, not being taken into account, and not having any impact in one's environment, which is experienced as non-existing.

Black Hole

Metaphor for an intolerably terrifying emptiness or invisibility as experienced by a person with a Lack of Sense of Self who doesn't feel like (they are considered) a "real" person. Like a force of nature, the Black Hole sucks in behavior and achievements that can potentially lead to approval. It fills itself with anything that serves as a Substitute Sense of Self, which immediately leads to anxiety about losing the Substitute Sense of Self.

Direct Motivation

Motivation that is ordinary, simple, and based in the present.

Direct Relationship with Self

A way of relating to your own being that includes body awareness, which means that you sense your Self without having to refer to achievements or other people's opinions about you.

Distorted Mirror

The process by which the primary caregiver is unable to effectively acknowledge their child(ren) as a separate being(s), as the caregiver is too wrapped up in their own problems and emotional neediness. The child inevitably and naturally concludes that he or she IS the way he or she sees him- or herself reflected by the caregiver, which is, in the light of the child's mind, an understandable but incorrect conclusion that can have far-reaching negative implications.

Early Childhood Survival Strategy (ECSS)

Conclusion to take refuge in gaining approval, drawn instinctively by infants/toddlers/children when their needs of feeling acknowledged as separate (unique) individuals by their caretakers are not met. This process becomes the foundation for an unhealthy way of experiencing the Self.

Ego-References

Subconsciously accepted requirements to feel and behave in certain ways and achieve certain results in order to feel approved of, as a substitute for a healthy way of experiencing the Self.

Enmeshment

An unhealthy relationship between child and primary caretaker. The child's identity remains under- or undeveloped and his or her motives stay geared toward getting the adult's approval, which leads to extreme dependence on approval.

Fear of Annihilation

Terror of being unheard by and invisible to others.

"Feel-good-about-self" (Fgas)

An emotional state (or thought) of relative well-being and safety based on the absence of feeling compelled to produce certain results at all costs, gained from succeeding to comply to the wishes of the caregiver, which leads to approval. It serves as a temporary and unhealthy substitute for a sincere sense of being alive (as a "real" person).

Focus Mode

Relaxed movements of the eyes, with the ability to stay fixed in the same place for extended periods, and which indicates a grounded mood or a person with a Healthy Sense of Self.

Healthy Sense of Self

The ability to experience and be present to your own person and to your own life and recognize both as uniquely owned by YOU. That includes the right to live and be as your Self and experience your innermost core as your ultimate home from where you live your life.

Hidden Agenda

A subconscious purpose that drives your actions or behavior, which is not the obvious, ordinary, expected purpose but the demonstration of the ability to perform an Ego-Reference to perfection, as a path to feel safe and on your way to achieving your Hidden Goal.

Hidden Goal

Your subconscious ultimate objective of getting the approval of your caregiver as an unhealthy substitute for feeling valued and related to (acknowledged) as a "real" person.

Hindrance

Any obstacle on your path to gaining a Substitute Sense of Self that frequently leads to anger or rage, which can be a gateway to violence or its counterpart, depression.

Indirect Motivation

The motive for doing or avoiding something is not what it appears to be; instead, the motive is to accomplish your Hidden Agenda and ultimately your Hidden Goal, which leads to a temporary emotional state that is the substitute for a lasting sense of being a "real" person.

Indirect Relationship with Self

Sensing yourself as a "self" through achievements or the responses of others, which gives you a temporary good feeling instead of a healthy abiding sense of being who you are.

Inner Conflict

Two or more competing and incompatible inner mandates to work toward experiencing a Substitute Sense of Self. This leads to high anxiety because the competition causes a no-win outcome.

Internalized Parental Voice (IPV)

The often-repeated verbal and nonverbal messages that parents, knowingly or unknowingly, transmit to their children becomes (almost?) hardwired in the child's mind so that it is perceived as an unquestionable truth (about and) by the child.

Lack of Sense of Self

Characteristic of a person who never developed a natural, ongoing inner knowing that he or she is truly alive as a "real," independent human being.

Magic Formula

A way of remembering the gist of the SoS Method: Move away from the addiction to "Feeling-good-about-yourself." First cross out the judgmental word "about" – don't be about your self – be yourself! Next cross out the word "good" – no need to point that out: good is your default state. What is left is: Feel your Self = sense your Self = have a Healthy Sense of Self!

Mirroring

The mutual and subconscious verbal and nonverbal processes by which the primary caretaker conveys basic feedback to the child about whether the caretaker relates to the child as independently existing individual or as a means to fulfill the caretaker's emotional needs – this message functions as a mirror for the child and is accepted as the truth of who the child is. The adequacy/inadequacy of the way this mirror functions is a decisive factor in the child's development (or lack thereof) of a Sense of Self of their own.

Motivation

In general, motivation is what creates an incentive or urge to do or avoid something. Motivation is the drive that determines behavior.

Motivation Check

A crucial (verbal) tool, which serves to a) detect your (Indirect) Motivation and b) record your Ego-References and Hidden Agendas, and to get insight what your Hidden Goal is.

Natural Sense of Self

The subconscious sense – developed normally in childhood – of being alive as a "real," definite person, with the unconditional right to exist as who you are, regardless of what others think, feel, or say about you.

Quality-of-Life Level

A healthy level of experiencing life's events and responding to them with emotional reactions that are in sync with the degree of intensity of the actual effect of these events or behavior of others on your life. It is indicative of a Healthy Sense of Self and distinguished from a (usually unaware) dependency on a Substitute Sense of Self where for the same type of events emotions are experienced that strike down to the level of your sense of existence-as-a-self.

Real Self/Authentic Self

The totality of one's body, mind, and emotions and what comes with being a person is experienced in the healthiest, most integrated way as an independent and autonomous being; actions and awareness are based on living experience, not contaminated by pathological motives. See also Natural Sense of Self.

Not so much meant in a spiritual sense but more as a reference to the whole person you really are.

Restored Sense of Self

The end result of working with the SoS Method, which is being healed from the dependency on a Substitute Sense of Self and which consists of a steady awareness of being one's very own person who is free to live life based on one's own essence, preferences, abilities, and limitations. There is an inner knowing of being separate from any parent or caregiver and free from any dependency on achievements or approval. There is an abiding sense of being (unconditionally) alive and "real."

Scanning Mode

A person's eyes moving around restlessly, searching for opportunities "to Score," which would fill the need for approval and "Feeling-good-about-themselves." Scanning mode use of the eyes indicates activity aimed at achieving an unhealthy way to experience one's self.

Sense of Self (SoS)

A conscious and/or subconscious awareness of existing independently as a unique and potentially autonomous human being.

Substitute Sense of Self

A psycho-emotional structure that develops as the artificial backbone of the psyche of those children/adults whose caregivers relate to their children as an extension of themselves, and that leads them to develop a compulsive drive for achievement-based approval.

To Score

Being successful in using a Vehicle to improve on an Ego-Reference; a success that feels like gaining points toward the Hidden Goal, which results in a "Feel-good-about-self" as a placeholder for the real-self experience.

The Hidden Goal does not necessarily always have to be parental approval. It also can be the undoing of early childhood traumatic experiences, such as being bullied, not being accepted by peers, etc.

Vehicle

An action, activity or behavior used to display the performance of specific skills or character traits rather than the obvious, ordinary goal. The performance is ultimately aimed at getting approval (Fgas).

The Twelve SoS Reconditioning Statements

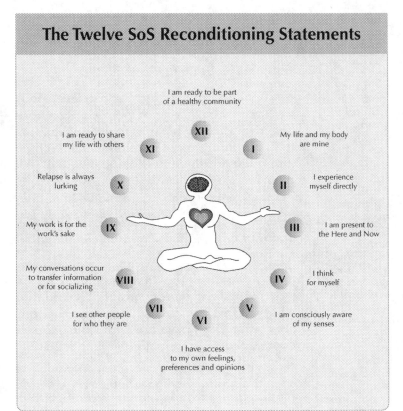

I am ready to be part
of a healthy community

XII

I am ready to share
my life with others

XI

My life and my body
are mine

I

Relapse is always
lurking

X

I experience
myself directly

II

My work is for the
work's sake

IX

I am present to
the Here and Now

III

My conversations occur
to transfer information
or for socializing

VIII

I think
for myself

IV

I see other people
for who they are

VII

V

I am consciously aware
of my senses

VI

I have access
to my own feelings,
preferences and opinions

The Twelve SoS
Reconditioning Statements

1. My life and my body are mine.
2. I experience myself directly.
3. I am present to the Here and Now.
4. I think for myself.
5. I am consciously aware of my senses.
6. I have access to my own feelings, preferences and opinions.
7. I see other people for who they are.
8. My conversations occur to transfer information or for socializing.
9. My work is for the work's sake.
10. Relapse is always lurking.
11. I am ready to share my life with others.
12. I am ready to be part of a healthy community.

* Quote from Antoinetta Vogel's book *Healthy Sense of Self, The Secret to Being Your Best Self,* Chapter 13, "Learning to sense your Self."

Benefits of a
Healthy Sense of Self

Less Stress & Anxiety

- Reduce your stress level, fear, and worry by staying true to your Self.

More Clarity & Focus

- Grow beyond approval-seeking habits, set your goals with intent, and define your own success.

Greater Self-confidence

- Build self-worth and recover the confidence that comes with being a creative, unique, and independent person: your true Self!

Emotional Intelligence

- Overcome self-sabotage and self-destructive habits as you begin relying on your Self for guidance.

Inner Freedom

- Learn how to look within to reach your personal and professional goals. Start living the lifestyle you deserve!

Deeper Self-awareness

- Recognize how your subconscious mind impacts the decisions you make. Learn what you can do to change your behavior to become the best version of yourself.

More Healthy Sense of Self Products

Read the Healthy Sense of Self Book

Become much more fulfilled in yourself and your relationships by restoring a healthy sense of self. In this book, Antoinetta Vogels shares how her journey to overcome insomnia led her on a path to self-discovery influenced by Eastern philosophy, traditional psychology, and self-reflection – through which she developed the **Sense of Self Method.**

https://healthysenseofself.com/product/the-motivation-cure/

What is the Sense of Self Online Course?

The Sense of Self Method Course

https://healthysenseofself.com/sense-of-self-online-course/

is a nine-week online training program designed to help you:

* Restore your Sense of Self, break free from the need to please others and get their approval.
* Develop the necessary skills to become your own independent person.

Learn to understand

- Why things are not working for you, why you do not get your desired results.

- What you have to do to make things better.

- How to work your way to a new, healthier direction and live from your own head and heart.

Staying true to your Self can be incredibly challenging if you never learned how. We here at HySoS guide you through a step-by-step program to get you in touch with who you truly are.

About the Author

Antoinetta Vogels was born in 1946 in the Netherlands at the end of World War II. She vividly recalls listening to her father's stories about the horrors of the war, while walking with him through the ruins of his native city, Groningen. She made the firm decision, even as a young girl, that she herself had to do something *to make wars stop*!

Little did Antoinetta know that life would offer her an opportunity to contribute to the understanding of human behavior by having her grow up with a "Lack of Sense of Self," and therefore providing her with the task of figuring out what was "missing" in her life.

As an accomplished bassoonist in several professional classical orchestras in the Netherlands, Antoinetta was a disciplined performer who enjoyed the creativity and expression of her work.

Motherhood resulted in two lovely daughters and the sudden onset of severe insomnia, which forced her into early retirement from her musical career early. This is where Antoinetta's inner journey began in determining the underlying cause of the predicament that continued plaguing her for over twenty-five years: insomnia.

Antoinetta started out with continuous introspection. Next she began recording her thoughts and feelings, a process that enabled her to identify patterns of behavior, and ultimately led to her Sense of Self Theory.

Antoinetta's mission is to share how a healthy Sense of Self is a crucial asset for each individual and for the world at large (Peace)!

Antoinetta lived in her homeland until 1995, when she moved with her family to Ithaca, NY. She later moved to Seattle, where she has been writing and speaking for almost a decade now.

Through her company, Healthy Sense of Self®, Antoinetta offers education and techniques that restore one's Sense of Self.

"A Healthy Sense of Self
is the backbone of the human psyche.
Without it a person skips his/her own life altogether."

Vision and Mission Statement of HealthySenseOfSelf®

Vision

Our Company strives to provide insight and deliver strategies that contribute to increase significantly the overall quality of life of the individual and ultimately of the world at large. HySoS helps in increasing or restoring a Healthy Sense of Self in the individual which immediately leads to improving health, productivity, success, well-being and peace. HealthySenseOfSelf® strives to expand this message in ever-increasingly diverse, effective, and well-utilized ways for ever-increasing numbers of individuals and groups so that this effect spreads outward in ripples, developing a momentum and life of its own.

Mission Statement

We believe that the world can be a better place and HySoS contributes to our envisioned world by developing and delivering both education and activities for making our Sense of Self healthier. Our specific ways of educating and providing activities for that purpose include, but are not limited to: offering information to individuals and to groups in the form of conferences, teleconferences, seminars and teleseminars, webinars online and/or real life –courses with potentially a Train-the-Trainers Program, educational speeches and presentations, podcasts, video's, radio and-TV appearances, articles in Journals, Newspapers and Magazines, a Newsletters, potentially our own Ezine. Our ultimate dream is: a HySoS –Foundation comprising of treatment and educational facilities, with national as well as international franchises.

HySoS strives to help people (re-)align with who they really are by strengthening or Restoring their Sense of Self®. Thus, we work specifically with parents, teachers, teacher-trainers, clergy, speakers, and others who influence many people, so we educate the educators for maximum scope of impact on the world. We also provide opportunities for both our employees and those we reach in other ways to gain full understanding and full benefits from this integrated non-medical method. We strive to be business as well as family, thus providing what's missing in many people's lives: a sense of purpose and home.

Overview HySoS Resources

Websites and Blogs:

https://www.healthysenseofself.com/

Website Netherlands:

https://www.gezondzelfgevoel.nl

Website Italy:

https://www.sanosensodise.it

Facebook:

https://www.facebook.com/Healthysenseofself

Facebook Netherlands:

https://www.facebook.com/GezondZelfGevoel

Facebook Italy:

https://www.facebook.com/SanoSensodiSe

Instagram United States:

https://instagram.com/healthysenseofself

Instagram Netherlands:

https://instagram.com/gezondzelfgevoel_nl

Twitter:

https://twitter.com/healthysos

Linkedin USA:

https://www.linkedin.com/in/annetvogels

Author's Amazon.com:

https://amazon.com/Antoinetta-Vogels/e/
B00JBFU1SG

Author of:

• *Healthy Sense of Self - How to be true
to your Self and make your world a better place*

• *Online Course: Introducing
the Sense of Self Method*

• *The Sense of Self Help! Workbook*

• *The Motivation Cure -
The secret to being your best Self*

- *A Guided Journal to a Healthy Sense of Self: Thoughts to Inspire Peace Within and Around the World*

- *How to overcome insomnia all by yourself*

Netherlands:

- *Gezond Zelf-Gevoel: Dé Methode om het beste uit Jezelf te halen*

- *Online Cursus: de Zelf-Gevoel Methode*

- *Werkboek voor de Zelf-Gevoel Methode (gebaseerd op de onlinecursus maar ook onafhankelijk te gebruiken)*

- *Het Gezond Zelf-Gevoel Dagboekje - Een inspiratiebron voor persoonlijke en wereldvrede*

- *Slapeloosheid - Hoe kom je er vanaf?*

Italy:

- *Sano Senso di Sé: Come liberarti dalla dipendenza d'approvazione*

- *Diario Guidato a un Sano Senso di Sé: 120 pratici suggerimenti per riconquistare la propria vita*

CONTACTS:

- Email: contact@healthysenseofself.com

Netherlands:
- Email: info@gezondzelfgevoel.nl

Italy:
- Email: info@sanosensodise.it

Printed in the United States
by Baker & Taylor Publisher Services